Firefighter Frida

by Vaishali Batra
Illustrated by Garry Parsons

Contents

Meet Frida! 2
Becoming a firefighter 3
Ready to help 7
Firefighter kit 9
The fire engine 10
At the fire 12
Other emergencies 16
Fire safety 21
Glossary and Index 24

Meet Frida!

"I rescue people in danger and teach about fire safety."

Frida

Frida is a firefighter. Firefighters put out fires. They help out in many other ways, too.

Becoming a firefighter

Frida completed a hard training course to become a firefighter.
It is a very tough job, so she had to do tests to show she was fit and strong.

Frida studied the science of fires.
She learned that a fire needs three things to burn:
- heat
- **fuel**
- **oxygen**.

A fire can be put out by removing one of these things.

Frida learned how to put out the flames. Most of the time firefighters use water. Water takes away heat by cooling the fire. Frida trained to use special equipment to fight fires.

Firefighters help at **emergencies** and accidents. Frida learned how to rescue people from cars and buildings. She learned how to give **first aid**.

Ready to help

A fire station has teams of firefighters called crews. When they are at work, each crew must be ready to help, day or night. At the fire station, firefighters check their equipment, do training exercises and keep fit.

There is a kitchen where firefighters can cook, and beds where they can rest. When a call comes in, the alarm rings. The firefighters must jump into action. There is a fire at a shop!

Firefighter kit

Frida rushes to put on her kit. It is waterproof and **fireproof**, so it keeps the firefighters safe from burns.

glow in the dark strips

protects the head from heat and falling objects

protects eyes from smoke and flames

fireproof trousers

The fire engine

Frida climbs into the fire engine. She turns on the loud siren and the flashing lights. Off they go!

A fire engine is usually a bright red colour.

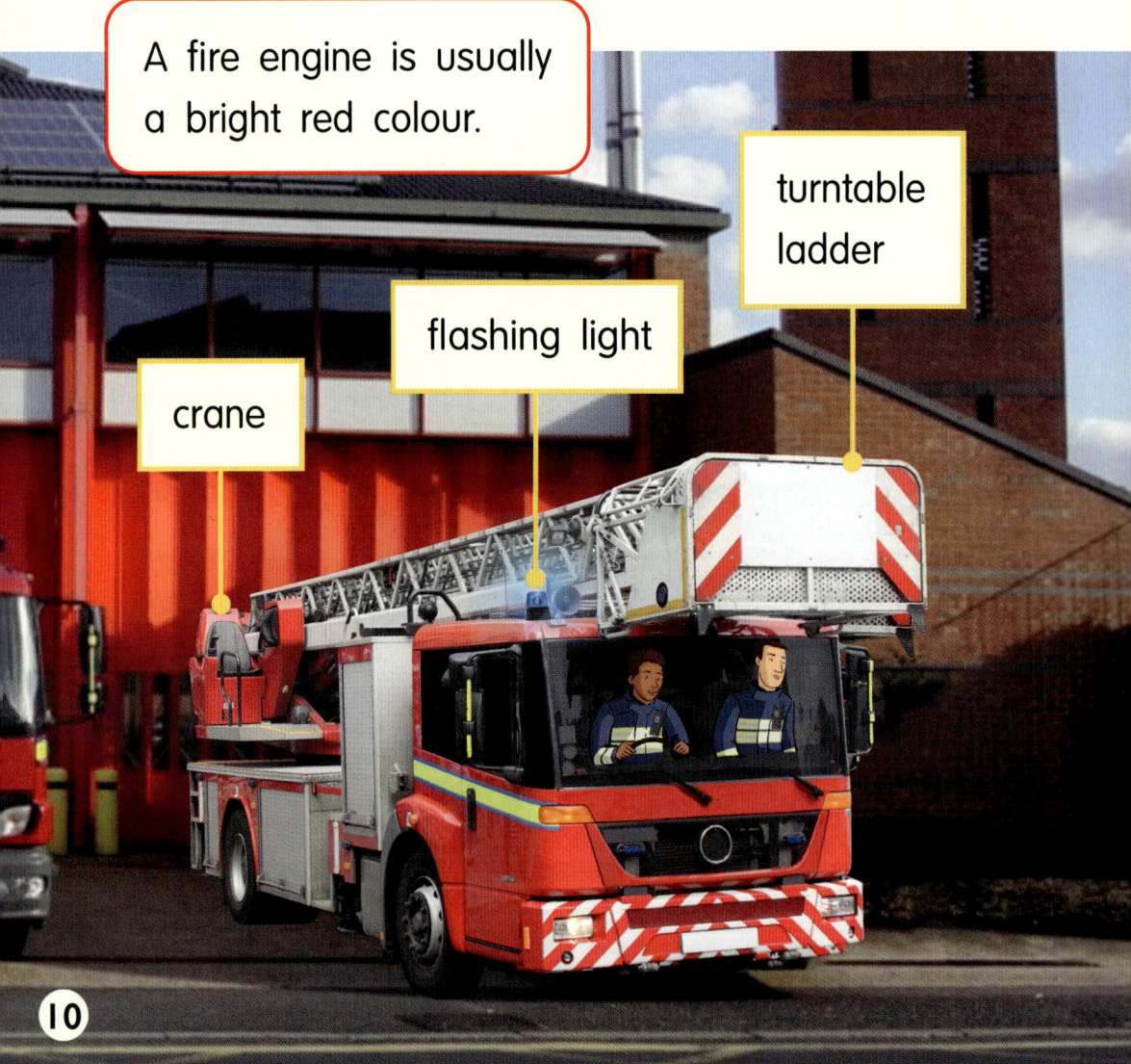

crane

flashing light

turntable ladder

Fires are dangerous, and they can spread very quickly. Firefighters need to get there fast. Cars move out of the fire engine's way when its lights and sirens are on.

At the fire

A fire can spread within a building very quickly. It can even spread from one building to another. A fire in this shop can easily spread to other shops nearby.

After a short journey, Frida and her crew arrive at the fire. There is so much heat and smoke! The firefighters use the long hose. The hose is very heavy, so the crew must work together.

The turntable ladder helps Frida get closer to the fire.

Frida works with her crew to stop the fire. She uses the fire engine's turntable ladder to direct water onto the flames. Her crew guides her when she is really high.

Frida and her crew take turns and help each other, so they do not get too tired. Finally, after many hours of hard work, the fire is out.

I am tired and my muscles ache, but I'm happy everyone is safe.

Other emergencies

Firefighters also help people who are in trouble in other types of emergency.

Floods

Floods can be very dangerous. People can become trapped as water rises. Firefighters wade through the flood water using poles and ropes to rescue people.

Flooding in Bangladesh

Bangladesh is a beautiful country in South Asia. It has many rivers and it gets a lot of rain. Flooding is very common and affects millions of people.

Firefighters rescue people in boats.

Forest fires

Sometimes firefighters are needed at a forest fire. They dig a ditch near the fire to stop the flames spreading.

A forest fire can be huge. It can take several days and many crews of firefighters to put one out.

Up in the air

In some countries, firefighters use helicopters to stop large forest fires. They drop thousands of litres of water on the huge flames to put them out.

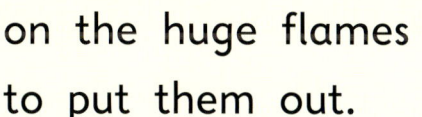

This forest fire in Australia spread across many kilometres of land.

Animal rescue

Firefighters also help animals that have got into trouble.

Fire safety

Firefighters are busy even when there is no emergency.

Home visits

Frida visits people's homes. She fits smoke alarms and checks that they work.

smoke alarm

Don't forget to test your smoke alarm once a month!

School visits

Frida visits schools to explain what to do in a fire:

- Shout "Fire! Fire! Fire!"
- Leave the building quickly.
- Call the emergency services.
- Do not go back inside.

Do not run or stop to collect anything.

Frida has a dangerous job. It takes a lot of courage to do it. She is a brave firefighter.

Glossary

emergencies: sudden dangerous events that need to be dealt with quickly

fireproof: unable to be damaged by fire

first aid: simple medical treatment that is given to an injured person before a doctor comes

fuel: something that is burned to make heat or power

oxygen: a gas in the air

Index

animals 20
fire 4–5, 11–15, 18–19
floods 16–17
training 3, 7